I0096576

BEGINNING AND ENDING YOUR NOVEL

WRITING LESSONS FROM THE FRONT
BOOK 15

ANGELA E. HUNT

HUNT HAVEN PRESS

The **Writing Lessons from the Front Series**

1. *The Plot Skeleton*
2. *Creating Extraordinary Characters*
3. *Point of View*
4. *Track Down the Weasel Words*
5. *Evoking Emotion*
6. *Plans and Processes to Get Your Book Written*
7. *Tension on the Line*
8. *Writing Historical Fiction*
9. *The Fiction Writer's Book of Checklists*
10. *Writing the Picture Book*
11. *The First Fifty Pages of your Novel*
12. *The Art of Revision*
13. *Writing Dialogue*
14. *The Business of Writing*
15. *Beginning and Ending Your Novel*

A Christian Writer's Possibly Useful Ruminations on a Life in Pages,
supplemental volume

———

The first ten books are available in one volume, Writing Lessons from the Front,
the first ten books.
Paperback ISBN: 978-0692311134
Hardcover ISBN: 978-1961394100

Visit Angela Hunt's website at www.angelahuntbooks.com.
Beginning and Ending Your Novel, Copyright 2024 Angela Hunt.
Published by Hunt Haven Press. All rights reserved. Do not reproduce or
share these pages without permission from the publisher.

———

ISBN: 978-1961394-858 (paper)
978-1961394-865 (ebook)

INTRODUCTION

Like the other lessons in the **Writing Lessons from the Front** series, *Beginning and Ending Your Novel* zeroes in on one topic—in this case, the all-important start and finish of your novel, short story, or screenplay. The principles here apply to any form of fiction.

If you're a voracious reader, at some point you probably picked up a novel and couldn't get past the first few chapters —the beginning didn't work for you. Or you may have invested hours in a novel and found the ending a terrible disappointment.

Strong beginnings *hook* a reader on the story and the characters; solid endings remain with readers long after they finish the book. If you create a strong beginning and a solid ending, you'll gain a reader who will eagerly sign on for your next book and maybe even the one after that.

So how do you write a strong beginning and a solid ending? This lesson will give you the insights and tools you need.

All writing tools build on one another, so we will be

discussing the plot skeleton, explained in the first book of this series, and repeating some concepts found in *The First Fifty Pages,* Book Eleven of the **Writing Lessons from the Front** series.

Let's get started!

1

THE BEGINNING

For our purposes, the beginning of a novel is the first act, if you divide your novel into three acts. If you have sketched out a plot skeleton, the beginning begins with the first scene and continues until the inciting incident, or about 20 percent of your novel. The beginning is the story from the first page until your protagonist leaves his ordinary world and heads into the story world.

Because it is easier to find movies we all recognize rather than novels we're familiar with, I'm going to refer to movie plots in this book.

In *The Wizard of Oz*, the beginning begins with the first moment we see Dorothy, the main character, and continues until the tornado sets her house down in the land of Oz.

In *The Sound of Music*, the beginning begins the moment we see Maria dancing in the mountain fields and continues until she enters the world of the Von Trapp family mansion.

In *Jaws*, the beginning begins with the opening shot of the beach until 22 minutes in, when the city council decides to hire Quint to kill the shark. The protagonist, Sheriff Brody, enters the world of shark fishermen.

In *Pinocchio*, the beginning ends when the puppet becomes a real boy; in *Peter Pan*, the beginning ends when Peter talks Wendy and her siblings to fly with him to Neverland.

In *Gone with the Wind*, the beginning begins with Scarlett flirting with the Tarleton twins and ends when war is declared and she enters the world of the Civil War.

The next time you watch a movie, note the time when the movie begins, then pay special attention around minute 22 or 23—in a movie of typical length, that's the point at which the main character will leave his ordinary world and enter a special world, the *extraordinary world of the story*.

Those first twenty or so minutes—or approximately the first 20 percent of your manuscript—is your beginning.

———

WHAT IS the purpose of the beginning? In the beginning, your job is to do several things:

- introduce the protagonist and encourage the reader to bond with him
- indicate the story's genre, tense, point of view, and the writer's voice
- reveal the era and setting of the story
- begin in the middle of an interesting problem for the protagonist
- resolve the protagonist's interesting problem
- show the reader what the protagonist really needs—his flaw, lack, or his hidden longing
- have the protagonist demonstrate admirable qualities
- display the protagonist's vulnerabilities

- establish important other people, places, or things in the protagonist's world
- include a hint about the end of the story
- and state the theme of the story.

See why beginnings are so important? That's a lot to do in a relatively short space. But if you do it well, your reader will stick with your protagonist to see what becomes of the character and if her hidden need (her flaw, lack, or hidden longing) is met at the story's end.

2

THE FIRST CHAPTER

As we move through this lesson, I'm going to present a hypothetical novel I'll probably never write. Let's say you've picked it up in the bookstore and opened it. Where are you heading first?

To the first page.

If you're like most people, you have flipped right past the title page, the copyright, and anything else before the first page of story. Yet many writers can't resist the urge to insert an author's note, a prologue, and acknowledgements in which they thank everyone from their spouse to their cat.

Your job as a novelist is to plunge the reader straight into the story, so why stop along the way?

If you need an author's note to explain why you adjusted a historical timeline or some other detail, put it at the back of the book.

If you want to thank those who supported you, take as many pages as you need at the back of the book.

If you want a dedication or an epigraph, keep it brief.

And why do you need a prologue? You may not need one at all. If you are *certain* you need one, keep it brief.

Whatever you do, *don't compensate for a slow beginning by stealing a scene from the ending* and putting it up front as a teaser. I know that's a common situation on TV shows, but there are better ways to structure stories. Don't steal from your climax to enliven your beginning—go back and create a stronger first scene.

If you have added a prologue for the purpose of including backstory, cut it. We're not going to put backstory in the beginning, because in this section of the book, we're interested in propelling the reader *forward*. Many writing teachers would join me in saying, "Backstory belongs at the *back* of the story."

Yes, there are exceptions to the "skip the prologue" rule. One is in the mystery genre, when a murder or other crime is often revealed in the prologue, and the first chapter opens with Mr. Detective, protagonist, reporting to work, where he deals with a problem in the office until he learns about the crime.

Another exception occurs when you wish to set the stage for your story. I crashed a plane at the beginning of my novel, *The Note.* The prologue was a brief scene written in omniscient point of view that showed various people getting onto the plane. But the reader doesn't enter the protagonist's head until chapter one.

So resist the urge to clutter up the front of your novel with stuff readers don't usually read. They want to get to the story, so let 'em get to it.

THE CONTRACT with Your Reader

Your first scene—your first chapter— establishes an unspoken contract between yourself and your reader. Without even knowing it, you are telling the reader several things about the book to come.

1. **The protagonist:** Your reader expects that the first character they meet will be the protagonist. If the character in that scene is not the novel's main character, your reader will be jarred when later they meet someone else who turns out to be the central character. Avoid giving your reader whiplash, and let us meet your protagonist in the first scene. Remember—good plot structure does not open with the main story event. You've probably heard that a novel should open "*in media res*," or in the middle of an action, and that's true. So show us your protagonist as she deals with an interesting problem in her "ordinary world."

In the introduction, I referred to the inciting incident when the protagonist enters a different world and sets off on an adventure. This should occur about 20-23 percent of the way into the story.

Have you ever seen an athlete throw a javelin? I'm no sports expert, but I've seen those athletes run down a lane, then they take a preliminary lunge before they make the throw. They initiate a smaller action before they give their all and throw the javelin.

I know that's an oversimplification, but it works as an analogy for story. You should open your story with a small action, an arc, that is preliminary to the larger action/arc that will become the main story problem.

Think back to *The Wizard of Oz*. In the beginning, before the tornado picks up Dorothy's house and drops her in Oz, Dorthy deals with a separate story arc—her dog has been eating Miss Gulch's flowers, so Miss Gulch demands the dog so she can take it to the sheriff. Dorothy, who lives with her aunt and uncle (nothing is ever explained about where her parents are, but there's clearly a problem), is horrified at the thought of losing her dog. She's so upset that she runs away from home and encounters a traveling fortune teller, who gazes into his crystal ball and pretends to see an older woman crying. Dorothy believes him and realizes she will hurt her aunt and uncle, so she returns home. One small story arc, one small hop that's easily resolved, but it's all preliminary to the huge arc that will unfold when Dorothy arrives in Oz.

If you need a review on plotting, see *The Plot Skeleton*, the first book in the **Writing Lessons from the Front** series.

Back to our contract with the reader.

2. The first scene and chapter also identify **the genre**. The reader may have already discerned the genre by the cover, but your first scene will settle any questions. It is either a romance, a western, a mystery, a thriller, a historical, or any of the many other genres represented in bookstores. (If your book fits in none of the standard genres, it will be marketed as "general fiction," which is not necessarily a good thing because it's not easily classified.) But your first scene will reinforce the reader's impression of the genre and give them a clue about what to expect in the rest of the book.

A genre romance, for instance, always has a happy ending. The guy and the girl *will* get together. In a murder mystery, the detective will solve the crime. In a thriller, the good guy will overcome the villain. Readers read genre fiction because they know what to expect. Break that rule at your peril—if you want to get a publishing contract.

3. Your first scene will also establish the novel's **tense and point of view**. Tense is easy—the book is either unfolding in past tense ("He walked to the store and looked around") or present tense (He walks to the store and looks around). Occasionally you may encounter a book that mixes tenses—for instance, a book in present tense may include a

flashback written in past tense. That's appropriate. But when not writing a flashback, writers should aim for consistency so the reader isn't confused.

Point of view is a little trickier. Stories are either written in omniscient (the God-view, where a narrator relates the story and knows everything), first person (*I went to the store*), second person (*You went to the store*), or third person (*He went to the store*). Occasionally you will encounter a novel where the protagonist is written in first person and all other characters are written in third person. Whatever POV you choose, make sure your pattern is consistent.

4. The first scene and chapter also establish the **writer's voice**. What is voice? There are dozens of highfalutin definitions of voice, but the reality is simple: A writer's voice is the way she puts words together. Each writer—indeed, each person on earth—has a way of speaking, a set vocabulary, and a way of phrasing words.

The other day I had a freak out moment while watching a YouTube video. I called my agent and said, "You won't believe this, but there's a YouTuber with your voice!" It wasn't the physical sound of the woman's voice that resembled my agent's, but her vocabulary, the rhythms of her words, the pauses, even the chuckles and laughter. My agent listened to one of the videos and agreed—the resemblance was uncanny.

In the same way, every writer has a voice. The more you write, the strength of your voice grows along with your confidence. As you study craft and become more experienced, your writer's voice will evolve, but it will always be yours. Writers who write purposefully, without fear, will have strong voices.

I've had people ask, "How do I discover my voice?" The only way to discover it is to write . . . a lot. Then sit back and read some of your work aloud. Then read someone else's work aloud, and notice how their voice—their rhythms, their vocabulary—differs from yours. You each have a distinctive voice.

I remember reading one of my manuscripts that an editor had tweaked—she had inserted the word *goon*, and I laughed. In all my years of writing, I've never used that word. Not that I have anything against *goon,* goons, or goonies, but the word just isn't part of my vocabulary. Not my voice, so the word stood out.

5. Your first scene and chapter will establish the **story world**. The reader will learn where and when the story is set, whether it's first century Rome or 25th century Mars. People in New York City speak differently than people in Atlanta, Georgia. People in Cuba *think* differently than people in the United States. Human emotions are the same no matter where or when you're writing, but the way people think, speak, work, and play can vary depending on their location, background, and worldview.

Your job in the beginning is to provide a look at the daily life and social mores in your story's time and place. You don't have to describe everything—show the *top* of the iceberg, not the entire chunk of ice. And you don't have to explain.

Without explanation, how do you avoid confusing your reader? Let's say that most homes in your fictional futuristic world have a *tublinatone*. I have no idea what that would be, but you can avoid explanations by *showing the tublinatone in action.* Maybe people bathe in it. Or eat on it. Perhaps it makes music when they breathe on it. Whatever you decide, don't explain it, but show people using the unfamiliar object or concept.

6. The first scene or chapter should give the reader **a**

hint about the ending. You can introduce an object that will have symbolic meaning, you can feature a geographical location that will be more meaningful at the end of the novel, or you can have a character utter a phrase that will have an entirely new meaning by the end of the story. But if you include a hint of the end in the beginning—and an echo of the beginning at the end—readers will feel a sense of completion when they close the book. They will have come full circle.

If you're familiar with the concept of "the hero's journey" from mythology, you'll remember that at the beginning of a story, the hero sets out on a journey. He receives a call to adventure, leaves his ordinary world and encounters a new world, sets a goal, encounters complications, experiences a bleak moment, makes a life-changing decision, and learns a lesson. He then takes his newfound maturity and knowledge and returns to his ordinary world to share what he has learned with others.

That's why it's good to hint at the ending in the beginning. You are quietly assuring your reader that things will be okay—or vastly improved—by the time the story is finished.

3

THE FIRST LINE

"The first line sets the tone, the melody. If I hear the tone, the melody, then I have the book." (Elie Wiesel, *Against Silence: The voice and vision of Elie Wiesel*)

After a person picks up your book and is intrigued by the cover, he or she will then flip to the first page. The first page is home to the first scene, which features a first line.

No sentence is more important than this one.

Rare is the writer who comes up with a winning first line on the first try. I usually write five drafts of a novel, and sometimes I'm still tinkering with that first line on the fifth draft. A first line needs to be so compelling that it hooks the reader and compels them to keep reading.

Here are a few guidelines:

- Avoid opening your novel with scenery.
- Avoid opening your novel with descriptions of rooms or furniture.
- Avoid opening your novel with a weather report.

I know, I know—you've probably read dozens of novels with first lines about scenery, description, and weather. And while I urge you to avoid those things, I didn't say you *can't* use them. But after you've read this section, compare your first line with descriptions of scenery to the first line you'll write after you've read this section. Which is *better*? Which would do a better job of hooking your reader?

Today's readers are different from yesterday's readers because we have many more things competing for our time and attention. We have email to answer, five hundred TV stations to watch, and movies streaming on our laptops, our phones, and even our watches.

Because writers face stiff competition, we need to grab readers from the first sentence.

I'm part of an online writers' group, and frequently one of us will say, "Time to play the first line game!" and everyone will post their first sentence.

Trouble is, a good many of those folks will upload two sentences, or even an entire paragraph. If you feel you need more explanation to accomplish the purpose of your first line, that sentence probably isn't pithy enough.

The best first line I *ever* read came from a Jodi Picoult novel:

Ross Wakeman succeeded the first time he tried to kill himself, but not the second or the third.

Wow. I *had* to keep reading. I don't remember what that novel was about, but I've never forgotten that first line. Why?

Let's analyze it: there's no scenery. No description. And no weather, not even a breeze.

What does it have? A person. People love to read about

other people because we are social creatures who love to eavesdrop on the lives of others. The line doesn't say, "Ross Wakeman lived in sunny California . . ."

Ross Wakeman isn't interesting because he exists or because of where he's living. He's interesting because he was trying to kill himself. Whoa. And, to sink that hook in the reader's psyche, Picoult adds that Ross succeeded the first time . . . but not the second or the third.

Wow. I have a half dozen questions in my head, and they are all clamoring to be answered. Why did Ross want to kill himself? If he succeeded the first time, who brought him back to life, and how? How did he try the second time . . . and the third? Why would he try again and again? And who is Ross Wakeman, anyway?

In Picoult's first line, we see the winning first line formula. To hook a reader right away, mention **a person**, then **raise a provocative question** in the reader's mind.

I once attended an intensive writing seminar led by Don Maass, well-known writer and literary agent. Each of us students had a novel-in-progress, and Don asked each of us to stand and read our first sentence aloud. Then everyone else had to raise their hand to show whether or not they'd keep reading.

Talk about pressure! Don started on my side of the room, so I stood up and read mine: *A grieving woman, I've decided, is like a creme brûlée: she begins in a liquid state, endures a period of searing heat, and eventually develops a scab-like crust.*

I nearly melted in relief when the others responded with smiles and uplifted hands. Why? Because I had introduced a person (the first-person narrator, who is clearly speaking from personal experience) and information that raised a question: What happened to this woman? Why was she grieving? Why does she have a scab-like crust?

Lots of writers begin with dialogue: *"Get out of here, you horrible man!" she shrieked.*

This leaves me cold, even though someone is shrieking. Why? Because I don't know this unidentified "she," and I have no idea why she's shrieking. More to the point, I don't care about this person because none of the words on the page placed me inside her head. What she says—"Get out of here, you horrible man"—may or may not be reliable, so it adds no dimension to the woman's character. I might be a little curious about why she found some man horrible, but life is short and lots of things are more interesting than this opening line.

If you open your story with dialogue, that opening comment needs to be powerful, fascinating, and compelling.

I have just returned from my bookshelves where I opened at least a dozen beloved novels to look at their first lines. None of them opened with dialogue—not one. That doesn't mean there *aren't* any novels that effectively open with dialogue, but I couldn't find any on my overcrowded shelves. So open with dialogue *only* if it's the absolute best option you have.

I asked some of my writer friends to send me first lines from their works-in-progress—I wanted some lines that didn't sound like me. Within five minutes, I had more than I could use, so here's a sampling:

> Savannah Daniels should have known the day would be upsetting the minute she saw old Boo Radley blocking the brick walkway to her classroom.

I like that a lot—but the writer's email included a note that Boo Radley is a gator, and that's wild! Because we want to keep that sentence rhythmic and as pithy as possible, I would tweak it like this:

> Savannah Daniels should have known the day would be upsetting the minute she saw the old gator, Boo Radley, blocking the brick walkway to her classroom.

See? We have a person, Savannah Daniels, who we automatically assume to be our protagonist. We also have a challenge: a gator, Boo Radley, is blocking Savannah's entrance to her classroom. What *is* she going to do? Plus, that sentence puts me in Savannah's head, because if seeing a gator is only "upsetting" for her, I admire her pluckiness. I'd be terrorized.

Another friend sent this one:

> Nightmares were supposed to stop once little girls woke up, but when five-year-old Scarlett Radcliffe opened her eyes, things only got worse.

I like this! I'm thinking Scarlett Radcliffe is the protagonist, probably as an adult, and this feels like a suspense novel. The only edit I might make would be to change the word "things" to something more specific: "the night only got worse." Or "her situation" only got worse. Or "she discovered her nightmare had just begun." (Words like "things" and "it" are often nonspecific, and specificity works better.)

Here's another:

> My gymnastics career ended with an injury—and I wasn't even the one who got hurt.

That line made me laugh. I can see that the "person" is the first person narrator, and I want to remain in her company because she made me smile. The provocative question, obviously, is who got hurt? And how in the world could that happen?

What about this one:

On July 4, 2019, a body floated just below the surface near the mouth of the Back River in Eastern Virginia.

This intriguing line reads like the beginning of a murder mystery. I'm not familiar with the story, but many suspense novels open with a dead body. The omniscient point of view presents a factual view of what's happening, but even this brief line includes a person—the body—and a provocative question: what happened to this person? And how did he or she come to be in the river? Also, notice the specificity of the date—the writer nailed it down in time, a murder on the Fourth of July. Interesting!

Another writing friend contributed this line:

It took one-ten-thousandth of a second—exactly 0.000169 seconds—for the bullet to rip through his shoulder.

I love it. Why? Because a person—a man—is getting shot. Why? I want to know. I also want to know how he knows the exact speed at which the bullet is traveling. He's clearly some kind of expert on gunfire and/or ballistics. And talk about specificity!

I'm not familiar with this writer's story, either, but I suspect that the point of view character is either the man getting shot or a medical examiner reviewing a body. If it's the latter case, I might tweak it by adding the medical examiner's name to put the reader in her point of view, like this: "Allison Wendel noted that it had taken one-tenth of a second—exactly 0.00169 seconds—for the bullet to rip through the man's shoulder."

But if the POV character is the man being shot, that line is perfect just as it is.

And one more:

Cemeteries always smelled of earthworms and damp dog fur, especially after a rain, and Brudge rather liked it that way.

Oh. My. Goodness. This is beautifully creepy, and though I don't know who Brudge is—or even if Brudge is a he or a she—I'm hooked. Who is this person, and why does he like the smell of cemeteries? Why do cemeteries smell of damp dogs? What has happened in Brudge's past? People aren't born with a love for rainy, smelly cemeteries.

So when you begin your novel, write your first scene and get on with the novel. Don't let your progress come to a complete stop over a single sentence.

But keep coming back to that first line. Polish it again and again. Run it past your friends. Cut words, add words, read it aloud and listen to the rhythm. Cut any extra syllables. Make the verbs unexpected. Add specific sound, smells, tastes. Make sure there's a person for the reader to care about, and a question that entices the reader to keep reading.

Practice makes perfect.

4

THE BEGINNING SCENES

Since nearly every new writer knows the first scene should start with some form of action, many begin the story with an explosion, a gunfight, a murder, or a kidnapping.

Those things are okay if you're writing a thriller or a western, but what if you're writing women's fiction? And even if you're writing a thriller about a child who is kidnapped, why should you *not* begin with the kidnapping?

Let me show you:

On a cloudy Friday morning, nine-year-old Louisa Jones's life changed at the corner of Wimple and State Street. She stood on the sidewalk, book bag in hand, waiting for the light to change. Without warning, a black van whipped around the corner and stopped, its door sliding open with a slam. A masked man jumped out, grabbed Louisa, and threw her into the van. The driver slammed on the gas, the van rocketed into the right lane, and the startled onlookers stared in horror.

Only when one of them noticed the girl's book bag on the sidewalk did someone think to call the police.

Nice first sentence, huh? Much better than the one I had in my first draft.

But this opening isn't nearly as effective as it could be because we don't care much about Louisa. How can we? We don't know her.

The average reader has read hundreds of stories about abandoned, abused, and missing children, and we've grown accustomed to the fact that evil exists in our world. We don't like it, but we are no longer horrified or shocked by it.

So how do we bring the horror of Louisa's situation to the reader?

Here's the technique: we create a "short hop" story arc that will do all the things we've outlined in the contract with the reader. The true purpose of this minor arc is to illustrate Louisa's character so the reader will care about her when the short arc ends and the main story problem begins.

So let's say Louisa wants to enroll in space camp for kids, and she thinks her dad might not let her because she's only nine. But she loves anything to do with space travel, and she wants to be an astronaut when she grows up. So she's trying to find the courage and the right time to approach her father.

And here's the backstory—which we're not going to write or explain, but we are going to *show*.

Three years before, while the family was on vacation in Florida, Louisa's mother saved six-year-old Louisa from a riptide, but couldn't get back to shore. She drowned, Louisa's father busied himself with work to avoid confronting his grief, and Louisa has been attended by a series of nannies. The family is wealthy and lives in a large urban city.

While we're constructing that plot, the reader needs to bond with Louisa. We need to help the reader feel her emotions. Because this is a kidnapping story, Louisa is going to feel afraid.

Because we are all former children, we should be able to remember how if feels to be afraid. So make a list of every occasion you can remember being afraid. How did you feel? How did you physically manifest fear? Did you bite your nails? Did your kneecaps wiggle? Did your heart pound? What did you do? How do you manifest fear as an adult? This exercise will help Louisa experience the same dread and fear you felt when you were young.

Now that we have a small story arc, instead of opening with the abduction, we open with Louisa in her ordinary world. She has a short-arc goal—space camp—and problems readers can relate to.

In this first scene, she's running late for school. How do you feel when you're running late?

Louisa pulled on her cardigan and stared into the mirror, then licked her fingertip and ran her damp finger over the rebellious cowlick near her forehead. Her mother used to do that, and Louisa never minded the touch of her wet fingers.

"Louisa!" A voice called from the bottom of the staircase. "Hurry up, you're making me late!"

Louisa sighed and looked for her shoes. One lay next to the bed, where she'd kicked it off the night before, but the other?

She dropped and peered beneath the bed. Nothing.

She stood and searched the closet. Nothing.

"Louisa!" The voice was more strident now. "For the last time, get down here!"

Louisa bit her lip, then remembered that Jasper had been in her room and the puppy had a thing for shoes. She slipped on her right shoe and padded down the hallway to the bathroom, where Jasper slept at night.

There—her left shoe lay in his bed, a little chewed, but not too much.

She slipped it on, patted the puppy's head, then ran back to her room and picked up her book bag.

"Louisa, I'm coming up there! You won't like it if I catch you!"

Louisa strode toward the door, then stopped to kiss two fingers and press them to the framed picture on her dresser. In the aging photo she and her mother stood on the beach, both of them smiling into the camera.

Louisa rushed toward the stairs, wondering if she would ever be happy again.

Okay—see how this short scene gives us some insight into Louisa's life? The woman at the foot of the stairs is obviously not Louisa's mother. She doesn't sound very kind or caring, and Louisa is intimidated enough not to yell back at the woman.

Louisa isn't causing a problem on purpose—anyone who has a dog has dealt with missing shoes, so the problem isn't the girl's fault. But it's distressing for Louisa because the woman keeps yelling, and it's also distressing for the reader. We feel for the kid, and when we see that she pauses to press a kiss to the photo, we realize something horrible has happened to Louisa's mother. The beach hints at the drowning, but this isn't fully revealed yet.

Notice that we did not take the time to explain anything —we didn't explain who the woman was, where and when the photo was taken, or what happened to Louisa's mother. Our job in the beginning is to *resist the urge to explain*, or RUE. Our task is to propel the story forward and create questions in the reader's mind. When we do that, we are creating tension, not of the mad bomber variety, but of *character*.

The woman downstairs grows ever more impatient with Louisa, but Louisa bears the woman's sharpness in silence. Will she explode? Will she remonstrate? Will she ever fight back?

Notice that there are no recollections or flashbacks in the scene. For our purposes, a recollection is a *brief memory that takes place in present story time*. A flashback is *a complete scene set in past story time*.

We could have inserted a recollection when Louisa paused to kiss the photo, like this:

> Louisa strode toward the door, then stopped to kiss her fingers and press her hand to the picture that stood on her dresser. In the aging photo she and her mother stood on the beach, both of them smiling into the camera.
>
> That **had** been the last time they visited Indian Rocks Beach and stayed at the little vacation house. Mom and Dad were happy, laughing and singing and swimming in the warm gulf. They **had** gathered shells and roasted marshmallows on the shore . . . a memory that remained with Louisa even now.
>
> Louisa rushed toward the stairs, wondering if she would ever be happy again.

Nothing technically wrong with that recollection, but even though it's short, the recollection stops the story in its tracks. The stop would be even worse if the memory had been longer. And why is it necessary? The reader doesn't need to know where they were staying, or that they roasted marshmallows. All the reader needs to know is that the woman in the photo is Louisa's mother, and that Louisa loves and misses her. And that information informs the reader about the woman yelling at the foot of the stairs. We don't know who she is—she could be a nanny, a distant relative, a housekeeper, or a stepmother—but we will drop other hints later.

Your goal in the beginning is to *purge all backstory*. I know that can be tough, but try to aim for no back story in *at least* the first thirty pages. You and your reader will be glad you did.

So if you've written your first draft, go through the first section and highlight anything that takes place, however short, *prior to the present story moment*. Then create a new computer file, name it "Cut backstory," and cut/paste your backstory sections into that file. I know it's painful to cut material, but you're not trashing it, you're simply stowing it somewhere else. It'll be there if you need it, but I'm pretty sure you won't.

Here's a tip about how to find bits of backstory in your text. Go to the "edit" menu and select the search/replace function. Search for "had" and replace it with "HAD" in capital letters. Now you're likely to see your backstory bits bookended by "hads."

Look at the example about Louisa and her mother on Indian Rocks beach. The proper way to introduce a recollection is by the use of "had"—you use one at the beginning of the recollection to take the reader back, and you use another at the end to bring the reader back to present story time. You only need two *hads*—you don't need to use past perfect tense throughout the recollection.

So cut the backstory, save it in your backstory file, and read your draft again. I'm betting that it reads better because the story is only moving in one direction—forward.

Don't worry—if you've cut explanatory material and you feel it's important, there are other ways to work it in—through dialogue, perhaps, or through exposition. But use those methods logically, and don't fall for the old "As you know, Bob" trap. If you have one character telling another character what the second character would already know, back up and start again.

If I had the woman at the bottom of the stairs saying, "As you know, Louisa, I've been your nanny for three years, ever since your mama drowned off that beach in Florida," — that's an "as you know, Bob." Kill it. You don't need it.

So how would you get some of that information across? Perhaps like this in the next scene:

When the BWM stopped at the corner, the woman behind the wheel stopped chewing her gum long enough to stare at Louisa. "What 'cha waiting for, kid? Outta the car."

Louisa unlocked the door, grabbed her book bag, and hopped out. She turned, about to say goodbye, but the BMW was already rolling, barely giving her time to close the door.

Louisa's friend Amanda waited by the bike rack in front of Starbucks. "Hey, Louisa."

"Hi."

Amanda cracked a gap-toothed smile. "How was the witch this morning?"

Louisa blew out a breath. "The same."

"How many nannies have you had since—you know."

"Four. Not counting this one."

"Wow." Amanda rummaged in her book bag, then pulled out a bag of fruit snacks. "Here. 'Cause I know you don't get sweets with your lunch." She waited until Louisa ripped the package open with her teeth, then grinned. "So? Did you ask your dad?"

Louisa popped a fruit snack into her mouth, then blinked. "About what?"

"Space camp. The deadline's next week."

"I know. But—" Louisa sighed. "I don't think he's going to let me. He'll say I'm too young."

"But Mr. Martin said you'd qualify 'cause of your good grades. And I don't want to go by myself."

Louisa looked up at the sky, where a scattering of cumulous clouds reminded her of last night's popcorn. "I'm going to ask," she said, lowering her gaze. "When the time is right."

"You better find the right time soon." Amanda crossed her arms over her book bag. "Because I can't go to space camp without my best friend."

See? You can give whatever explanations you need in present story time. Just *keep the story moving forward.* There will be a time for looking back—and a reason to do it—later.

5

THE READER-CHARACTER BOND

As a novelist, your job is to create a bond between the reader and your protagonist. Before we discover how that can be done, let's refresh our knowledge of story structure.

The beginning of your story is your opportunity to develop your character so the reader willingly goes with the protagonist into what can be a frightening and unfamiliar new world. In order for the reader to agree to the adventure, you need to create a bond between your reader and your protagonist.

If I wanted the protagonist of my book to be a detective, I would open the story with a scene from the detective's point of view. He would have been dealing with a problem—maybe he gets an emergency call and his car won't start—and I would include details to reveal *his* character and hint at his backstory.

If I wanted the protagonist of this kidnapping story to be the girl's worried father, I would open the book with a scene from the father's point of view. He would be dealing with an interesting problem and a small goal—perhaps he was robbed of his wallet by a thirteen-year-old hoodlum, which sends him to the police station to complain about rising crime while oblivious to the danger awaiting his own daughter.

But my plan is for Louisa to be a bright, admirable girl who engineers her own rescue from the diabolical kidnappers. In order to make this idea credible, in the first 20 percent of the story I have to provide the reader with evidence that Louisa *could* do this. In an 80,000 word book, that means I have about 16,000 words, or around 64 pages to show that Louisa is capable, smart, and resourceful.

So I need to construct scenes that demonstrate those qualities while she pursues her small-arc goal of persuading her father to let her attend space camp. I have to write scenes that show her vulnerability. I have to introduce suspects who could engineer this kidnapping. I have to introduce the significant people in her life—her father, the nanny, her best friend, her favorite teacher, the boy she likes best, and her beloved dog.

I have to lay the groundwork for the villains, give them a reasonable motive for the kidnapping, and hint at what they are capable of doing if her father doesn't pay the ransom. I need to introduce a few "red herrings," or likely suspects—the nanny is a natural for this role, since I've already painted her as unlikeable.

But most important, whether the main character is the detective, the father, or the kidnapped girl, I have to make the reader fall in love with my protagonist. How?

1. Make your protagonist **vulnerable**. It's easy to make a child vulnerable, but what if your protagonist is a strong, capable man? Most police procedurals and movies exploit the detective's vulnerability by threatening someone he loves—his wife, his family, or his dog.

You could also make your protagonist vulnerable by

giving him a physical handicap—debilitating migraines, for instance, blindness, deafness, or a broken leg. The vulnerability could be permanent, or something that comes and goes. But your protagonist must have a vulnerability. Even Superman has kryptonite.

2. Make your protagonist **admirable and competent**. Give him a noble nature. Give him physical and/or moral strength and convictions. Make her virtuous or spiritual. Give her a special talent or ability, something no one else can do as well as she can. Make this gift surprising—a strong man who saves abandoned kittens or a woman who can fix a car faster than the neighborhood mechanic.

Even antiheroes have to be admirable in some way. In *The Godfather,* Don Corleone ran a crime syndicate and had people murdered, but he had a code of ethics—his organization refused to sell drugs. Bad for the kids, they said. And while you're creating an antagonist or villain, remember that he needs a good reason for doing the evil he does. His evil machinations may not make sense to the rest of the world, but they must make sense to your villain.

4. Give your protagonist a **flaw**. It doesn't have to be huge —it could be as simple as a tendency to do things halfway. Or perhaps he tells one little "white lie." Or she betrays one friend. Whatever it is, this flaw or weakness will eventually come around to bite them, and they'll learn a lesson. We all have flaws, and we've all learned from them. Your reader will identify more easily with a less-than-perfect character than a superhero.

5. Give your protagonist a **sense of humor**—especially if it's self-deprecating. If you're creating an interesting, gifted, smart character, give them a little humility to counteract all those strengths. Let her shrug off her victories. Let him sincerely celebrate when others win. Allow his best friend to

point out his weaknesses and failings. Make your protagonist fully human. If you're familiar with the Myers-Briggs personality profiles, give him a type and you'll be able to research his strengths and weaknesses in a flash. The writing lesson *Creating Extraordinary Characters* has tips on how to do this.

6. Give your character **a hidden need**. Not a trivial flaw, the hidden need should be deeply emotional and usually the result of a wound in the protagonist's past. This wound may not be easy to spot—after all, it's hidden—but you should drop hints and provide evidence that it exists.

Example: In *The Wizard of Oz*, Dorothy is on the farm living with her aunt and uncle. Nothing is ever said about Dorothy's parents, but it's not normal for kids to live with their aunt and uncle unless something has happened to Mom and Dad. This is implied, not spoken, and in the beginning it becomes clear that Dorothy is not happy on the farm. She wants to be somewhere, anywhere else.

But after spending time in Oz, and after being thwarted from going home, she comes to appreciate the farm, Uncle Henry, and Aunt Em. She is able to accept that she now belongs on the farm; it's her home. So she can say, "There's no place like home," with true feeling.

Now picture a circle with points at the top and bottom. The top point represents the beginning of the story, and the bottom point represents the end. The right side of the circle can represent the plot movement, and the left side the character growth.

A good story has both an active plot *and* active character development, but some stories place more weight on one side than the other. *Steel Magnolias* is a character story about a woman, M'Lynn, who struggles to save her daughter's life while depending on the support of her friends. The plot is centered on all the things she does while trying to save her daughter (stop the wedding, stop Shelby from having children, arranging for a kidney transplant), and the character growth is centered on how M'Lynn learns to deal with letting her child go her own way . . . and learning that life goes on.

Most James Bond films are heavily weighted on the *plot* side of the circle. James works against impossible odds to save the world from a nefarious villain while barely changing his character . . . except in the last few Daniel Craig movies, where he's actually been allowed to express emotion.

Try to make sure both sides of the circle are well-represented in your novel. By the end of the story, the hidden emotional need you've portrayed in the beginning should be met and the wound healed. Your protagonist is now changed for the better, and will never struggle with that hidden need again.

7. Finally, recall your own experiences and **transfer your past emotions** to your characters. How did you feel when your best friend discovered you'd leaked the secret you promised not to tell? How did you feel when your mom forgot your birthday? How did you react when you didn't win a ribbon at the county science fair? How do you react when you're in a hurry and your car won't start? Let your protagonist feel those feelings and your readers will relate to your character. Because at one time or another, they've felt the same emotions.

Remember Dorothy's small story arc at the beginning of the Wizard of Oz? Consider the reasons we bond with her in the first part of the story:

1. We see that she's loyal, brave, and sacrificial. She fights for her dog, Toto, and would willingly go to bed without supper for him.

2. She's vulnerable. She's living with her aunt and uncle, with no sign of her parents.

3. She's virtuous—we see her being kind and friendly with the farm hands, who are obviously fond of her.

4. She's talented—in the movie, she sings beautifully.

5. She's devoted to her family—when she runs away, all Professor Marvel has to do is point out that Auntie Em is crying, and Dorothy hurries home. She doesn't want to hurt anyone.

6. She has dreams and longings and feels emotions fiercely. She's passionate.

7. She has a hidden need—she needs to feel that she's home.

If you've been wondering how you're going to fill those blank pages, here's your answer: Create scenes and situations in which your protagonist reveals virtues, weaknesses, a hidden need, talents, dreams and goals, and vulnerability. Help him or her strive toward a small goal, encounter a couple of problems, and overcome them. Then they'll be ready for the inciting incident, which will escort them into the main story problem.

If you can do those things, you will have given your beginning everything it needs to appeal to a reader.

6

THE BACKSTORY

A fully-fleshed character has a backstory: the sum total of the life events that have shaped him or her to become the person he or she is. So as you work on your novel, ask yourself this question: What was the single most transformative event in my protagonist's life before chapter one?

For Louisa, my young protagonist, it would be her mother's drowning on their family vacation. Louisa is nine years old when the story opens; the drowning occurred when she was six. Six is old enough to remember a catastrophic event.

If I had chosen the father or detective as the protagonist, I would have many more choices because the adults have lived longer than Louisa. Perhaps the father's most formative life event was when he defied his father and chose to go to law school instead of taking over the family business. That disagreement has colored his family relationships ever since.

Perhaps the detective's formative event occurred when he was thirteen and his best friend was hit by a car. The reckless driver was never identified, so since then the detective has yearned to "set things right." His loss changed his life and directly influenced his decision to join the police force. It still influences him so he's a hard-nosed cop, determined to arrest and convict no matter what.

Once you've decided on a formative event, ask yourself how lessons the protagonist has learned will affect him as your story unfolds. Since we're going to avoid backstory in the beginning of the novel, once your hero has entered the special story world (after the beginning), use the beginning to drop hints about that past event. Later, probably around the three-quarter point of the novel, you can insert a flashback and give us an entire scene depicting that event as it happened in your character's past. Don't shortchange it by making it a brief recollection. Give us the entire scene, complete with sights, sounds, tastes, textures, and raw emotions.

Your reader will now understand why your protagonist feels, acts, and reacts the way he or she does . . . because they, too, have lived through that transformative event.

But don't drop this flashback into the beginning or the early part of act two. Save it for the moment your protagonist is about to face the biggest challenge of his story. After the flashback scene, he will *own* the memories, emotions, and lessons of that life-changing event, broaden his shoulders, and charge forward to win or lose.

There is a time—late in the story—for backstory. But it needs to be *significant* backstory, not meaningless details.

I'm not saying that you can use *only* backstory for a transformative event—our lives are changed by myriad meaningful moments, and you can use any of them once you're past the beginning. If writing about adults, consider the moments they fell in love, got married, got divorced, grieved a death, suffered disappointment, won an unlikely victory, or became a parent. Memories from any of those or similar events will deepen character when you allow us to experience them through the eyes of your protagonist. So feel free to delve into your characters' pasts to allow the reader to realize why your characters are the way they are. Just try your best to keep all those memories, recollections, and flashbacks out of the beginning.

Everything in your novel should do one of two things: advance the story forward or deepen character. If an element isn't pulling its weight, cut it and stash it in a file. You don't need it, and you probably won't miss it.

Your reader certainly won't.

7

APPROACHING THE ENDING

Once you have written a great beginning, write the inciting incident, have your protagonist establish his (film-able!) goal, and create interesting complications to stand in his or her way. Following the plot skeleton, have those complications "curve" from positive to negative, to even out your pacing—too many bad things in succession will weary your protagonist and your reader.

How many complications should you have? It all depends upon whether you're writing a short story, a novel, a screenplay, and how long you want the work to be. The minimum, however, is three. I use the plot skeleton to write children's picture book, and they have three complications. My novels can have a few dozen complications. Everything depends on the pace of your story, your genre, and your intended audience.

However many complications you have, note that they should become more and more challenging. Your protagonist tries and succeeds, tries and fails. He burns bridges, suffers loss, and wins some victories. Then, when success is closer than ever, something terrible happens—the worst complication of all, and it leads to the bleakest moment—the point of no hope.

This is where your ending begins. It's Act Three, if you want to think in a three-act structure. Act Two is all about complications, people, events, and developments that stand in the way of your protagonist's pursuit of his goal. But once your protagonist hits the biggest obstacle, the worst event that leads to his bleakest moment, you're at the threshold of your ending.

Now—time to write a solid ending that will satisfy your readers and keep them coming back for more.

So let's get back to the story. You need tension at the beginning of your ending, and the way to get it is to have the complications increase in difficulty. When you sit down to plot out your skeleton, make a list of all the possible complications, then rank them in difficulty from least to most difficult. Save the most difficult for the last challenge, and let it lead to the bleakest moment. This moment must be a true trial that will end in despair and impending defeat. Your protagonist must face the limits of his courage, resolve, and abilities—that's how you keep your reader reading, because the reader wants to see how your protagonist overcomes this ferocious obstacle.

At the bleakest moment, your character can't help himself. His friends can't solve the problem for him. He's well and truly stuck in despair. So how does he get out?

Let's look at Dorothy again. All she wanted was to go home to Kansas, but she's had to travel through a foreign and freaky land, she's been poisoned, and she's nearly been killed by a witch, but she's found friends and laughter and she's seen things she never knew existed. Then she meets the wizard, who happens to have a hot air balloon, and he happens to be from Kansas himself! He says he will take

Dorothy home and she's on board, but then her beloved dog jumps out to chase a cat, so Dorothy climbs out to catch Toto, and while she's retrieving him, the wizard and his balloon rise into the sky and fly away . . .

And Dorothy is stuck in Oz. Her three friends can't solve her problem, or they would have already have done so. She needs help from above and she gets it when the Good Witch Glenda comes down in her bubble mobile.

Glenda tells Dorothy that she's had the power to go home all along. Dorothy is incredulous, and the Scarecrow asks Glenda why she didn't speak up earlier. And Glenda says, "Because it's a lesson she had to learn for herself."

And then, in the most on-the-nose writing possible, the Scarecrow says, "What'd you learn, Dorothy?"

And Dorothy states the lesson learned: "I learned that the next time I go looking for my heart's desire . . . I'm not looking any farther than my own backyard."

Satisfied that Dorothy has learned her lesson, Glenda says, "All you have to do is click your ruby slippers together and say, with feeling, 'There's no place like home.'"

So Dorothy hugs her friends goodbye, holds tight to Toto, closes her eyes and *decides* to go home. She clicks the ruby slippers together, says the words, and awakens in her own bed . . . and she's happy to be back on the farm.

Her hidden need is met.

In that scene are all the things you need to write a solid, memorable ending.

But *The Wizard of Oz* is a children's story, so let's look at a story for adults. The elements we will look for are:

- the bleakest moment
- the helper
- the lesson learned

- the decision made
- the resolution . . . to show that the character has truly changed.

The other day I rewatched the ending of *Terminator*. Sarah Connor, the heroine, and Kyle Reese, the man sent from the future to protect her, spend most of the movie running from the Terminator, a cyborg sent from the future to kill Sarah because her future son will lead the resistance against the computers who rule the world. Kyle and Sarah are nearly killed, but they finally manage to maneuver the Terminator into a fiery crash. But he emerges from the flames as a metallic skeleton, still intent on accomplishing his goal.

But Kyle manages to insert an explosive into the Terminator's midsection, at the cost of his life. The Terminator explodes, and we think the cyborg is dead . . . until the upper half of the torso inches toward Sarah and tries to choke her.

Sarah, who at the beginning of the movie was a disorganized, unskilled woman who knew nothing about computers, draws upon everything Kyle has taught her and manages to lure the remaining half of the terminator into a machine that finally destroys it. Against all odds, this once-fragile human woman defeats a cyborg from the future. Her *bleakest moment* was when the torso kept coming despite Kyle's death, her *helper* was Kyle's courageous example, and she *learned* that she could not give up because the future of humanity was at stake. She *decided* to persevere and keep fighting.

The last scene of the movie, the *resolution*, shows a pregnant Sarah at a gas station in Mexico, where a young boy takes a picture of her. She is speaking into a tape recorder, recording her story for the unborn son she knows will become a future freedom fighter. A man at the gas station warns her that there's a storm coming, and she says, "I know," as she thinks about what's to come. She is a changed woman, and will live her life differently because she met and fell in love with Kyle Reese . . . and because she encountered the Terminator.

Even though Kyle dies in the movie, we know he willingly gave his life because he fell in love with Sarah and he loved their son, John Connor. We appreciate the ending because Sarah changed into a warrior who will lead the fight against the malicious machines.

Think about the ending you want to write. Do you have the appropriate plot "bones" in place? Before you do anything else, make sure those are present.

8

THE BEGINNING IN THE END

Where does *The Wizard of Oz* begin? In Kansas.

Where does the story end? In Kansas.

Dorothy has come full circle, but the journey has changed her in many ways.

I finished a book on Sarah last week, and my opening line was this:

> Since I had agreed to marry my grandfather's choice, I stood in his chamber and waited, my faith minuscule and my confidence nonexistent.

I wanted to include a hint of the beginning in the end, but I couldn't have Sarah return to the place where she lived at the beginning of the novel because that would contradict history. I couldn't have her look the same because she had aged from thirty-nine to 127 years old.

So I chose to echo my first line in the last Sarah scene:

> As a camel snorted in the distance, I thanked ADONAI for His goodness to Abraham . . . and to me. In blessing my

husband, the Lord had abundantly blessed me. My faith had been minuscule, my confidence nonexistent, but even then, the Lord had granted me grace, honor, and more love than I deserved.

You might have a rough idea of your ending when you start writing your novel, and if you don't have to worry about being historically correct, you can start and end at the same place . . . or with the same song playing on the radio . . . or as the same comet blazes across the sky. Even if you don't know how your story is going to end, you can find something to echo or repeat in your ending.

Your reader will not recognize your "hint" in the beginning because they haven't read the ending. They may not remember enough of the beginning to realize that you have deliberately echoed words or a situation. But subconsciously, the reader will sense that you have come full circle and closed the story. And they will feel satisfied.

So whether it's in your first draft or your fifth, look for something in the beginning that you can repeat or echo in the ending. Perhaps it's a comment that restates the story theme, or perhaps it will be a location where something significant happened.

When *Gone with the Wind* opens, Scarlett is flirting with two young suitors outside Tara, the plantation where she grew up. At the end, she is sadder, wiser, and living in an Atlanta mansion, but what does she tell herself? She'll go home to Tara, the place that gives her strength. The book feels complete because Scarlett will return to the place where the story began.

As you begin to conceptualize your ending, think of your beginning. That's your starting point.

TYPES OF ENDINGS

The most common type of ending—and, arguably the most satisfying—is the **happily ever after** version. We grew up with fairy tales that end happily—unless you're reading the original versions, which are pretty grim. But in nearly all stories, the love interests get together, the hero achieves his goal, and all ends well.

I was thinking about Clint Eastwood's *Gran Torino*, one of my favorite movies. It's the story of a racist, foul-mouthed older man who is alienated from his grown children. Not a very appealing character, but we get to know Walt as the movie unfolds. He's a Korean War vet, and when a Hmong family moves in next door, they remind him of the war . . . yet they win him over. He decides to help them, and determines to make a man out of the teenage son. Ultimately, Walt has to come up with a way to permanently take care of the bullies that are harassing and abusing this family and their son. After settling his affairs, he sacrificially gives his life for them. It's a sad ending, but Walt changed, achieved his goal, and the Hmong family is saved. It's the saddest happily-ever-after movie I've ever seen, but it's wonderful.

Sometimes, however, the hero pushes toward a goal and then refuses it. For instance, in my novel *Afton of Margate Castle*, a young girl is used and abused by the lady of the manor, who marries her off to a horrid brute. After suffering terribly, Afton vows revenge on Lady Endeline, and works hard to be sure the woman pays for her cruelty. But as the years unwind, Afton matures, finds love, and comes to appreciate God's mercy . . . so when she is given an opportunity to take her revenge upon Lady Endeline, she shows mercy instead. Which makes for a happier ending.

Sometimes your protagonist does *not* win his goal, or even if he does, he realizes that the prize isn't what he really wanted. At the end of his story, he is **sadder but wiser,** like Scarlett at the end of *Gone with the Wind*. She spends the entire book pursuing Ashley, then realizes that it's not Ashley she loves, but Rhett, who has grown tired of butting heads with her. So he goes off to make peace with his relatives and Scarlett goes home to Tara. She's sadder and wiser, and we hope she won't make the same mistakes again.

Some writers create **open-ended stories**, where the protagonist wraps things up and moves on, not sticking around for happily ever after. The old movie *Shane* comes to mind, also the Clint Eastwood film *Pale Rider,* where he plays the personification of death. Death comes to town, exacts retribution, and moves on. This character does not change, but he creates havoc in the lives of everyone he meets.

Some writers opt for **twist endings**, which come in a variety of forms. Sometimes the ending features an *identity reversal*, where we finally realize that the protagonist is not who he says he is. One of the best known is *The Sixth Sense*, where the viewer realizes that the protagonist, Malcolm, is not only *not* who he says he is, he's not who he *thinks* he is.

He thinks he's a psychologist struggling with his distant wife; he discovers that he's a ghost only a gifted child can see.

Other twist endings include the **motive reversal**: the protagonist wants one thing, but chooses something else. The classic example is *Casa Blanca*. Rick loves Elsa, and at the end of the movie he is preparing to run away with her. But it's wartime, and he knows she'll be better off with Victor, her husband. So he sends her away with Victor, and tells her, "We'll always have Paris"—the place where they were together before the war.

Some stories end with a **perception reversal**—the world of the story is not what it seems. *Planet of the Apes* (the original) comes to mind. A man lands on a planet after a journey of hundreds of years in space, finds it inhabited by civilized apes, and struggles to survive. But at the end of the story, he discovers that he didn't land on a different planet, somehow he landed on Earth—and over time, the apes ascended to primacy. In the book, the protagonist escapes the apes who want to use him for experimentation, returns to planet Earth, lands . . . and is greeted by an ape deputy sheriff. Same shocking ending: the apes conquered humankind.

Another excellent perception reversal is found in the book *Rebecca* by Daphne Du Maurier. The protagonist, a sweet young woman, marries Max, a wealthy widower. They are happy until they return to his ancestral home, a mansion called Manderly, which seems to be haunted by Rebecca, Max's first wife. The housekeeper loved Rebecca, who was beautiful, talented, intelligent, and all the things the new young wife is not. Max seems to be haunted by Rebecca, too. The new wife is miserable in her new home and marriage until she finally discovers that Max didn't love Rebecca, he *hated* her because she was a scheming witch.

(She even arranges her death so Max will be blamed for her murder). An amazing story and well worth reading if you're interested in seeing how a perception reversal is done.

You might want to consider a **reversal of fortune** ending: the wealthy protagonist discovers that she has lost everything, or the poor protagonist discovers that she's entitled to a fortune. This reversal can be used as a general plot, but it also works well as an ending. Any poor girl who marries a prince will find her fortunes reversed (as in *Cinderella* or *Pretty Woman*), or a rich man who finds himself poor usually ends up humbled and/or imprisoned.

Finally, there's the fulfillment reversal, where a character thinks they have won, but the protagonist proves that they actually haven't. These endings are common in movies with super heroes—the villain gleefully declares that he has conquered Metropolis, but the hero steps forward and reveals that he has prevented the villain's victory through a clever move. A non-superhero example is *Silence of the Lambs*. Clarice Starling's boss and his jubilant team go off to arrest a suspect in several vicious murders while Clarice, on her own, knocks on the door of someone she suspects . . . and must survive an encounter with the real murderer.

Think back over some of your favorite movies—especially those with surprise endings—and identify which kind of ending it is. Happily Ever After? Sadder but Wiser? Reversal of fortune? Reversal of Motive? Perception Reversal? All of these are open to you, but not all of them will work for every plot.

10

WHAT TO AVOID IN YOUR ENDING

While some elements are important for your ending, other elements should be avoided.

First—avoid cliffhangers with the main character. It's fine if you don't settle a storyline with a minor or peripheral character—in fact, some writers use those minor characters and unsettled story lines to write sequels in the series.

But do not leave your protagonist with an **unresolved story line**. You should tie up all the lose ends in his plot.

Do not employ a **deus ex machina.** The term literally means "god from the machine," and it's derived from the Ancient Greek plays. They used to create all kinds of complications, but instead of solving them organically, they'd have a god literally rise from the stage to set things to rights. (The Greeks had a plethora of gods from which to choose.).

Today's writers don't employ Greek gods, but they can be tempted to use gimmicks and surprise devices. For instance, once I was reading a novel where the protagonist fell into a pit. The villain loomed over the pit and confessed to all his evil deeds, then told the good guy farewell.

As I recall, the next scene featured the good guy out of the pit (with no explanation of how he got out), then he pulled a tape recorder out of his pocket and pressed the play button. Everyone in the room then heard the villain confessing to all his evil deeds . . . and I wanted to toss the book into the trash. Not only did the author cheat by not explaining how the protagonist escaped an inescapable pit, but we didn't know he had a tape recorder in his pocket. The situation was entirely too convenient, a deus ex machina if ever there was one.

Don't do that.

Don't end your story too abruptly. You won't have to worry about this if you have all of the plot skeleton pieces in place, but if *Terminator* had ended with Sarah Connor pressing the button to kill the terminator, that would have been too abrupt an ending. Movie patrons would have left the theater wondering what happened next. Make sure you take your characters through the bleakest moment, helper, lesson learned, decision made, and resolution. The resolution is a scene or two where you show the reader how the character has changed . . . and we realize that the protagonist is going to be okay.

Don't have your protagonist **move on without resolving all the plot threads of his story**. We've all seen movies where the mysterious stranger who came to town wanders off alone, but he'd better wrap up his complications before he leaves.

Do not have the **helper—whoever it is—solve the protagonist's problem.** What if Glenda the Good had come down, whirled her wand around Dorothy's head, and sent her straight back to Kansas? Dorothy wouldn't have learned anything—or at least the reader wouldn't know anything about it.

What if Kyle Reese had pushed the button that killed the Terminator? He would have been the hero, not Sarah, and she had to be the one who grew into the courageous Sarah Connor, the woman who taught John Connor to be a warrior and a fighter.

Make sure your protagonist solves the problem, not his helper or anyone on his team.

11

WHAT READERS WANT IN AN ENDING

Readers want an ending that leaves them **feeling rewarded** for investing hours of their life into a book. Time is the currency of our lives. It's the one thing you can't buy and you can never get back once you've spent it. So write a story that will leave your readers feeling as though their investment of time was worth it.

If you're writing a novel of **genre fiction—romance, thriller, mystery, western, etc.—make sure you understand the conventions of that genre.** In a genre romance, the guy and girl always get together. Always. A Nicholas Sparks hero may die, but he doesn't write genre romance.

In a mystery, the detective always solves the crime. He always announces the guilty party at the end, and he never relies on a clue the reader knew nothing about. Mysteries are a game played between the reader and the detective, so don't have your detective conceal a clue. That's not playing fair.

In a thriller, the good guy always defeats the villain. He may not always apprehend and arrest the villain, but the villain either goes to jail, dies, or limps away in defeat.

Whatever your genre, read other books in the genre so you'll know the conventions readers expect.

Readers want **emotion in their endings.** I've been in a couple of book clubs, and I never give a book a five-star rating unless it makes me cry. Novels are all about evoking emotion, and if I'm not moved to tears at least once, the writer has let me down. And it's not hard—I'm the sort who cries at Publix commercials, so I'm not asking a lot. So make sure there is emotion in your ending—great joy or grief or angst or anger or whatever's appropriate for your story. Your reader wants to feel that emotion, too.

Readers want **endings that make sense.** Characters should make logical decisions in keeping with the personality you've developed for them. A girl who did nothing but sit inside the house and read cannot suddenly pick up a bow and arrow and shoot the bear threatening her family. You're going to have to show her at archery practice in a previous chapter to pull that off.

Readers want **endings that tie up the loose ends** for their protagonist's story. You don't have to solve every problem for every character, but do take care of your hero or heroine.

Readers want **a resolution, a follow-up scene** to demonstrate the character's change. For Sarah Connor, it was sitting in the car, prepping for the coming war. For Dorothy, it was being happy back on the farm, telling her family—and the farm hands—how much she loved them. Give us a scene where we see the protagonist doing, saying, and thinking things he or she wouldn't have done, said, or thought before the story.

Sometimes you may want to add a **summary ending,** which requires *two* endings. For instance, in my book about Sarah, in the final scene Sarah dies and goes to meet

Adonai. But because I knew readers might appreciate some follow up about Abraham, I added another scene where Abraham bargains for the family burial ground, and an epilogue, where I matter-of-factly summarized Abraham's other children and their descendants. The book was Sarah's story; she was the character who changed most, but you can't really talk about Sarah without thinking about Abraham.

There's one more important element of a solid ending—**the visual element.** A novel can range from 50-100,000 or more words, and readers aren't going to remember those words—they're going to remember the *pictures* your words created. They're going to remember Scarlett O'Hara vomiting up the radish she found in the garden, all that remained after the Yankees ravaged her home. They're going to remember Sydney Carton standing behind the guillotine, comforting a seamstress, also condemned to die.

So don't just create an ending with introspection and dialogue—choose a memorable setting, unusual weather, any elements that can create a striking image. Once you've painted a memorable image, write those all-important last lines.

12

THE LAST LINES

If we work hard on creating our first line, why would we give little thought to the last lines of the book? They are important, too, but in a different way. Instead of trying to hook the reader, the purpose of the last paragraph is to impact the reader. To leave an imprint on her heart and mind. To be memorable.

The last paragraph is a place to echo the theme . . . or remind the reader of the lesson learned. It could be a quip or a quote that is imbued with new meaning at the end of your story.

So ask yourself: What emotion do I want my reader to feel at the end of this story? Satisfaction? Humor? Joy?

If your story is not a "happily ever after" tale, you should at least give your reader *hope*.

My novel, *Uncharted*, is about a cast of characters who are swept off a ship and awaken on an odd desert island. One of them realizes that they are dead and the island is Hades, the waiting room before Judgment Day. Pretty bleak, right? So how did I end that story?

The female protagonist has a teenage daughter who

wasn't on that sinking ship. So my protagonist determines to save her daughter at all costs, and at the end of the story, that's what she's trying to do. I had to give her—and my reader—*hope* in the face of an unchangeable situation.

In *Gone With the Wind*, Scarlett frequently says "I'll think about that tomorrow" when she's faced with a problem. And the last line of the novel? *After all, tomorrow is another day.* This line reinforces Scarlett's personality and implies that she'll be successful in winning Rhett's love again—after all, she's done everything else she set out to do.

Let's look at some other endings and consider what emotion the author wants the reader to experience.

Francine Rivers' *Redeeming Love* is the story of Angel, a prostitute who is loved and married by a Christ-like farmer, Michael Hosea. She struggles to accept his love, but when she finally does, her life is transformed and she takes the name *Sarah*. The last paragraph:

> After sixty-eight years of marriage, Michael died quickly. Sarah followed within a month. According to their wishes, only simple wooden crosses marked their graves. However, a few days after Sarah's burial, an epitaph was found scratched into her marker: Though fallen low, God raised her up. An Angel.

My book, *What a Wave Must Be*, is a heart-rending story of suicide and how it affects lives. The grandmother tells the story. The last paragraph:

> Frank and I *had* lived a charmed life, filled with undeserved blessings, until God planted a lesson in the soil of a difficult season and allowed us to water it with our grief.

Already I could see the glimmer of new life emerging from the broken soil.

Dean Koontz's *The Darkest Evening of the Year* is the story of Amy, Brian, and a special golden retriever. The novel features a summary ending, and concludes with this paragraph:

Too many dogs continue to be abused and abandoned—one is too many—and people continue to kill people for money and envy and no reason at all. Bad people succeed and good people fail, but that's not the end of the story. Miracles happen that nobody sees, and among us walk heroes who are never recognized, and people live in loneliness because they cannot believe they are loved, and, yes, Amy and Brian were married.

George Orwell's *Animal Farm* was required reading when I was in high school, and maybe it should be required again. It's the story of farm animals who rebel against an evil farmer, then set up their own society. Soon the pigs are in charge . . . and here's the last paragraph:

Twelve voices were shouting in anger, and they were all alike. No question, now, what had happened to the faces of the pigs. The creatures outside looked from pig to man, and from man to pig, and from pig to man again; but already it was impossible to say which was which.

William Kent Krueger's *The River We Remember* is a murder mystery centered around a river and the people in its vicinity. The book has a literary tone, and the author gives us a summary ending—a double ending—to update us on the lives of all the people involved. And the last paragraph:

> And so, she sips her whiskey and reads her books and every once in a great while allows herself the pleasure of a cigar, and she awaits without fear her own passing, when she will be lowered into the soil of black Earth County and laid to rest forever beside the moonlit, milk-white flow of the Alabaster, a river she remembers fondly as an old friend.

Charles Dickens' *A Tale of Two Cities* is a classic story about two men who look remarkably alike, one good, one not-so-good. The good man, Charles Darnay, is arrested and scheduled for execution; after an attack of conscience, the other man, Sydney Carton, comes to visit the jail, renders Darnay unconscious, and takes his place. Why? Because he loves Darnay's wife, Lucie. He saves Lucie's husband for her sake.

The last lines are poetic, beautiful, and memorable. Omniscient narrator Dickens tells us what Carton would have been thinking, and concludes with this: "It is a far, far better thing that I do, than I have ever done; it is a far, far better rest that I go to than I have ever known."

One more example: Gary D. Schmidt's *The Wednesday Wars* is a brilliant coming of age story. Set in 1967, the book's main character is seventh-grader Holling Hoodhood, who struggles with, well, growing up.

The book's first line:

> Of all the kids in the seventh grade at Camillo Junior High, there was one kid that Mrs. Baker hated with heat whiter than the sun.

(Of course, that kid was Holling). The books's last paragraphs:

> I guess you want to know what Mrs. Baker did when Lieutenant Baker came off the plane. And I guess you want to know what Lieutenant Baker did when he saw Mrs. Baker on the tarmac.
>
> But toads, beetles, bats. If you can't figure that out for ourself, then a southwest blow on ye and blister you all o'er.
>
> Because let me tell you, it was a happy ending.

Many of the above books leave the reader with hope. Other authors left the reader with a smile . . . or a simple appreciation for life and love. *Animal Farm's* message is a warning—beware of socialism, fascism, and communism, because the authoritative leaders will inevitably submit to the same temptations that flawed the former leadership.

All of the above endings leave the reader with a sense of *completion*. The protagonist has taken his or her journey, learned a lesson, and been changed. And now the story is finished.

As is this lesson.

So go write a great beginning, a wonderful middle, and a memorable ending. The world is waiting for your story.

13

EXERCISES

1. Which type of ending will work best for your work in progress? Why?

———

2. The most important way to be sure you have a solid ending is to find the "plot skeleton" bones—are they in the proper place?

Which is the **complication** that will lead to the bleakest moment? Is it dire enough to lead your character to a place of no hope? What will happen if he doesn't get help?

The person or creature who **helps**—does this person solve the problem, or does she simply give your protagonist a nudge or push in the right direction? The latter is what you need.

What **lesson** does your character learn? How do you impart this lesson to your reader? Does your protagonist say it, think it, or demonstrate it? If he demonstrates it, are you certain the lesson will be evident to the reader?

What is the **decision** made by your protagonist? How does he escape his problem? Is it something he could not have done at the beginning of the story? Kudos if it is, because that will demonstrate his character change.

What **emotion**(s) will your ending elicit from your reader? Will your reader be laughing, crying, cheering, or all three? What did you write to elicit that emotion? Let someone read your book or your last scene—did your test reader feel that emotion? Why or why not?

Did you include a **hint of this ending** in your beginning? If you didn't, can you find a way to put a hint of the ending in your beginning . . . or a hint of your beginning in this ending?

Finally, what **resolution** scene did you create to show that your protagonist's life will be different from this point forward? How will she incorporate the lesson learned into her daily life? How will he reap the benefits of what he has learned?

———

3. Create three different "last paragraphs" for your novel. Test them out on three different readers. Which is most effective?

———

4. Which type of ending did you choose for your story? Happily ever after, sadder but wiser, or one of the twist endings? Does this ending suit your genre? Is there another type of ending that might have worked just as well or better?

———

5. If you chose a "sadder but wiser" ending for your story, how did you give the protagonist—and your reader—hope?

ABOUT THE AUTHOR

Angela Hunt writes for readers who have learned to expect the unexpected from this versatile writer. With nearly six million copies of her books sold worldwide, she is the best-selling author of more than 165 works ranging from picture books (*The Tale of Three Trees*) to novels and nonfiction.

Now that her two children are grown, Angie and her husband live in Florida with Very Big Dogs (a direct result of watching *Turner and Hooch* too many times) and many chickens. Her affinity for mastiffs has not been without its rewards—one of their dogs was featured on *Live with Regis and Kelly* as the second-largest canine in America. Their dog received this dubious honor after an all-expenses-paid trip to Manhattan for the dog and the Hunts, complete with VIP air travel and a stretch limo in which they toured New York City. Afterward, the dog gave out pawtographs at the airport.

Angela admits to being fascinated by animals, medicine, unexplained phenomena, and "just about everything." Books, she says, have always shaped her life— in the fifth grade she learned how to flirt from reading *Gone with the Wind*.

Her books have won the coveted Christy Award, several Angel Awards from Excellence in Media, and the Gold and Silver Medallions from *Foreword Magazine*'s Book of the Year Award. In 2007, her novel *The Note* was featured as a Christmas movie on the Hallmark channel.

When she's not home writing, Angie often travels to teach writing workshops at schools and writers' conferences. And to talk about her animals, of course. Readers may visit her web site at www.angelahuntbooks.com.

www.ingramcontent.com/pod-product-compliance
Lightning Source LLC
Chambersburg PA
CBHW052026030426
42335CB00026B/3297

* 9 7 8 1 9 6 1 3 9 4 8 5 8 *